SUNKEN CITIES

T0328032

Contents

Written by Abbie Rushton

Collins

1 The myth of Atlantis

Who created the myth of Atlantis?

Plato was a great thinker and writer. He lived in a city called Athens in Greece. He was born around 428 **BCE** and died around 348 BCE. He wrote about lots of different subjects, including maths, politics and love. He also wrote about an island called Atlantis.

statue of Plato

The beginning of Atlantis

Plato's story of Atlantis started with Poseidon. He was the Greek god of the sea, **earthquakes** and **floods**.

Poseidon fell in love with a woman who lived on an island. He married her, then built a city and a grand palace for his wife.

Poseidon made his eldest son king of the island. He also used his son's name – Atlas – to create the name of the new island: Atlantis.

Did you know?
It was said that Poseidon also named the sea after his son – the Atlantic Ocean. It is still called that today.

statue of Poseidon, San Andrés island, South America

What was Atlantis like?

Plato described Atlantis as an island which was surrounded by rings of sea and land. These rings were designed to protect them from **invaders**.

There were lots of green fields where the Atlanteans (people who lived on Atlantis) could keep animals, and they had fresh water to grow **crops**.

They could also catch fish from the sea, so they had plenty of food.

The capital city glittered with gold and silver. It was full of beautiful temples, fountains and statues.

Atlantis had a large army and strong defences from attack.

What happened to Atlantis?

The Atlanteans were rich and powerful. They had everything they needed to live peacefully on their own island: food, water and money. But they became greedy. They began to invade other places.

When the Atlanteans battled against the Athenians (people who lived in Athens), they were defeated.

Plato said that the gods decided to punish the Atlanteans for their greed. They created earthquakes and floods which devastated the island. It sank into the sea and was never seen again.

artist's impression of Atlantis

2 Where might Atlantis be?

In 1882, Ignatius Donnelly, a writer and politician, published a book which claimed that Atlantis was a real place. Since then, many scientists, historians and explorers have tried to find Atlantis.

Plato said that Atlantis was "beyond the pillars of Hercules". One of these pillars is the Rock of Gibraltar. The other is probably in Morocco.

There are lots of places Atlantis could have been, but the main suspects are: Santorini, Greece; Malta, the Mediterranean; Azores, Portugal; Souss-Massa, Morocco; Strait of Gibraltar.

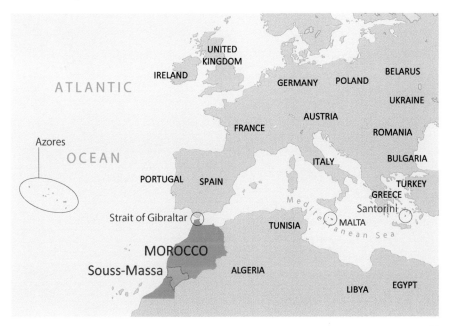

• Santorini

Santorini is the place most commonly associated with Atlantis.
There are several volcanoes on Santorini. It used to be one island but volcanic eruptions have split it into several smaller islands.

Santorini – photo taken from the International Space Station

Around 1600 BCE, there was a huge volcanic eruption on Santorini. It was probably the largest eruption ever seen by humans. It caused the volcano to collapse into the sea, creating an enormous **tidal wave** and leaving the ring shape we see today.

Did you know?

The effect of the eruption on Santorini was felt worldwide:

- In China, there was yellow fog and blackouts when the ash blocked the Sun.
- The poisonous gases released probably reached Africa.
- It is thought to have caused the temperature to drop around the world.

A group of people called the Minoans lived on Santorini in the Bronze Age (about 3000 BCE to about 1100 BCE), thousands of years before Plato. The Minoans lived in a place called Akrotiri. It was buried in ash during the eruption.

When **archaeologists** began to dig it up, they found lots of evidence about the Minoans. It seemed that they were very rich and powerful, just like the Atlanteans.

wall painting from Akrotiri showing an expedition

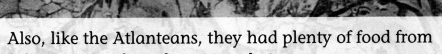

Also, like the Atlanteans, they had plenty of food from fishing, animals and growing their own crops.

However, no bodies were found in Akrotiri, and no valuables or jewels. This suggests that they had time to leave, which doesn't match Plato's story that it was an "unexpected punishment" that killed off all the Atlanteans.

• Malta

Malta has some of the oldest buildings in the world. Some are even older than the pyramids in Egypt and Stonehenge in England. This shows that there were humans living there from a very, very early age – between 3600 BCE and 2500 BCE. It also shows that these humans were clever, just as Plato described the Atlanteans.

There is evidence that Malta was joined to Sicily by a strip of land which has now sunk underwater. One possible reason for it sinking could have been an event like an earthquake or flood, which matches Plato's story.

All in the name ...

Some people believe that the clue to Atlantis's location is in the name. The early Greek language was written from right to left, and the letter "s" in Greek looks a lot like an "m", so what do you get if you write "Malta" backwards and swap the "m" for an "s"?

Atlas! The name of Poseidon's son.

What do you think? Do you believe that too?

ancient limestone buildings in Malta

13

• Azores

The writer and politician
Ignatius Donnelly first
suggested the Azores
as a possible location
for Atlantis. Some people
thought the islands could
be the mountain tops
of Atlantis.

There is a lot of volcanic
activity in the Azores.
This matches Plato's
description of floods
and earthquakes, which
were probably caused by
a volcanic eruption.

Underwater,
the land slopes steeply down
to a flat area, which could
have been the site of the city.

However, scientists have shown
that it couldn't have been the Azores
because the flat part has been underwater for
millions of years. Also, the volcanic activity means
that the islands are actually moving *up* out of
the water, so they're definitely not sinking.

Azores

15

• Souss-Massa, Morocco

Morocco isn't an island, but some people argued that Plato's word for "island" could also mean an area surrounded by oceans, lakes and mountains.

The mountains in Souss-Massa are the Atlas Mountains, which could be an important clue. They make a natural circle around the plain (flat area at the bottom), which could have been one of the circles that Plato was describing.

Souss-Massa plain in Morocco

This area has some **prehistoric** ruins. These were cut into black, red and white rocks, which sound similar to what Plato described. Souss-Massa was also close enough to the sea to have a **harbour**, which meant the people could fish, just as the Atlanteans did.

3 Was Atlantis real?

There were lots of devastating earthquakes and floods like Plato described, so it is possible that an event like this *could* have happened. However, that doesn't make the myth true. Sadly, most scientists agree that Atlantis wasn't a real place.

Also, Plato was the only person to ever write about Atlantis. If it had been a real place, surely more writers would have written about it?

It's likely that Plato invented Atlantis so he could create a story to warn people about being greedy. What do you think?

page from Plato's *Dialogues* where he wrote about Atlantis, 9th century

4 Real sunken cities

Despite the fact that Atlantis has never been found, there are lots of examples of amazing *real* sunken cities.

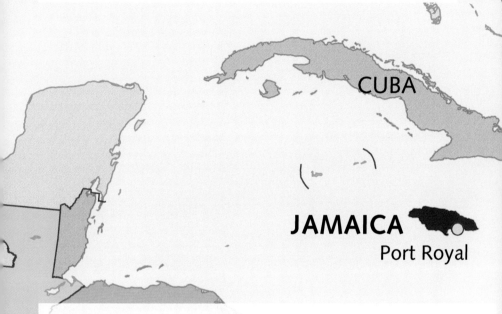

CUBA

JAMAICA
Port Royal

Port Royal, Jamaica

Jamaica was captured by England in 1655. Port Royal became one of the largest English settlements outside of Europe. It was also full of pirates! It was even ruled by a pirate called Henry Morgan from 1675.

On 7th June 1692, a massive earthquake ripped through Port Royal and two-thirds of the city fell into the sea. 2,000 people were killed.

ATLANTIC
OCEAN

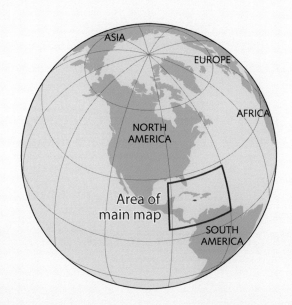

THE
BAHAMAS

AITI   DOMINICAN
REPUBLIC

PUERTO RICO
(U.S.A.)

ANTIGUA AND
BARBUDA

ST KITTS
AND NEVIS

DOMINICA

CARIBBEAN
SEA

ST LUCIA

ST VINCENT AND
THE GRENADINES   BARBADOS

GRENADA

TRINIDAD
AND
TOBAGO

Today, Port Royal is one of the world's most important underwater historical sites. There are more shipwrecks there than you'd find in any one place in the world.

Most of the remains of Port Royal lie under very shallow water, making them easy for archaeologists to study. They can see a lot of buildings and even whole streets!

One of the most amazing things that archaeologists have found is a pocket watch made in 1686 which had stopped at 43 minutes past 11, the exact moment the earthquake struck.

23

Dunwich

Dunwich is often described as "Britain's Atlantis". Today, it is a small, quiet village in Suffolk, but in the 11th century, it was one of the largest and more important towns in England. Battered by violent storms, the cliffs of Dunwich have been **eroded** and much of the town has slid into the sea.

It's too dark for divers to see anything beneath the waves at Dunwich, but a research team used sound waves to create an image of the seabed. They have found several ruined buildings.

This is called the "last grave" of Dunwich. It's all that remains of a graveyard that has fallen into the sea. The gravestone is just metres away from the cliff edge so who knows how much longer it'll be there.

Shicheng

If Dunwich is "Britain's Atlantis", Shicheng is "China's Atlantis".

Shicheng, or "Lion City", is about 1,300 years old. It was deliberately flooded in 1959 to create an artificial lake which would help to make power. After that, it was forgotten, until the Chinese government arranged for divers to explore it in 2001.

The water has protected Shicheng from damage
by the wind, rain and sun, helping to preserve it.
The divers found an enormous city with five entrance
gates, 265 arches, and beautiful carvings of lions
and dragons. They could even see wooden stairways
and beams.

Shicheng, China

Baiae

The city of Baiae in Italy was built in a volcanic area. This meant that hot water full of minerals came out of the ground. People came to bathe in the water. Baiae was like a spa resort for rich people. Some of the most famous Roman emperors visited, including Julius Caesar and Nero.

statue in Baiae

However, in the 8th century, Baiae was attacked, and in 1500, people left after a **malaria** outbreak. Because of the volcano's eruptions, the abandoned city gradually sank into the sea.

Tourists still visit the city of Baiae today, but now they have to use diving gear to see it! They will find countless statues, **mosaics** and carvings.

diver looking at a mosaic floor in Baiae

5 Exploring sunken cities

Less than 20% of our oceans have been explored. Think of all the amazing treasures that could be discovered in the remaining 80%!

But how do scientists, historians and archaeologists explore something as large, dangerous and unpredictable as our oceans?

Satellites

Sometimes the easiest way to see what's beneath the waves is to look from above. Satellites are spacecraft that float above the earth. They can take photos which show unusual shapes or structures under the sea.

Some people have joined the search for Atlantis from their own homes! Using satellite maps on the internet, they think they have found lost cities. These look like grids on the seabed. However, scientists say that these grids aren't real. They're an illusion created by putting a picture of one map on top of another.

satellites like this take pictures of Earth from space

Sonar

Dolphins use sonar – or sound navigation – to learn what's around them underwater. Humans can use the same technique. By bouncing sound waves off the ocean floor, they can build up a picture of what's down there.

When archaeologists found part of an Egyptian god's head in the sea not far from Egypt, they knew that it was part of a much larger site. The water was dark and they couldn't see very well, so they used sonar to help them. They made a map of the city of Thonis-Heracleion, and it helped them learn where to look for more treasures.

A statue of the God Osiris, found in the sunken city of Thonis-Heracleion.

Submarines and robots

Submarines are a safe way of exploring very deep water. They might have cameras or metal arms to help underwater explorers. But sometimes the explorers need a little more help.

This is a robot called Ocean One. It is designed to look and move like a human. It has fingers for grabbing. The person controlling it can even feel what the robot feels!

The first time Ocean One was tested in
an archaeological site, it explored the wreck of
La Lune, King Louis XIV's ship, which sank in 1664.
No human has ever touched the ruins or the treasures
inside them. Ocean One was able to pick up a small
vase, which was then sent to the surface.

Ocean One

Divers

Sometimes the best way to search for underwater treasures is with the human eye. Lots of divers have discovered ancient ruins.

Lake Atitlán, Guatemala, is the deepest lake in Central America, so it's no surprise that it holds some secrets. Diver, Roberto Samayoa, accidentally discovered one of them in 1996. He grew up near the lake and his gran had told him stories of a sunken church.

At first, Samayoa just found pieces of pottery, but these little things led to the discovery of something much larger – a Mayan city: Samabaj. "No one believed me, even when I told them all about it," Samayoa said.

Scientists think that it was once on an island in the lake, which flooded, possibly after a volcanic eruption.

Lake Atitlán, Guatemala

a bowl found in Samabaj

6 When myths become reality

Geologists are people who study the history and structure of Earth. Patrick Nunn is a geologist at the University of the Sunshine Coast in Australia. When asked about Atlantis, he said: "I don't think there's any question that the story of Atlantis is a myth."

But Patrick Nunn believes that there may be other myths which relate to real events and places. This is called geomythology – the study of geology and mythology.

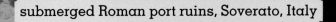
submerged Roman port ruins, Soverato, Italy

Nunn tells a story from the Solomon Islands, near Australia. A man was so angry when his wife ran away to live on another island that he bought a magic curse. He followed his wife and planted two plants on her island, keeping a third plant for himself. When the leaves appeared on his plant, the curse said that his wife's new island would be swallowed by the waves.

Back on his own island, the man stood on a mountain and waited until leaves appeared on his plant. Then he watched as his wife's new island sank beneath the sea.

The island is a real place, and it did sink underwater. It's not possible for waves to have sunk it, but an underwater earthquake could have done so. The island was at the edge of a slope, so when the earthquake struck, it slid into the depths of the ocean.

Solomon Islands

Another famous place which was described in myths and legends is the city of Troy. Homer wrote about the war on Troy in *The Iliad*, a very famous and old poem.

Many people believed that – like Atlantis – Troy was just a myth and didn't exist. Until Heinrich Schliemann, a German archaeologist, went looking for it in Turkey … and found it! In fact, what he found led to the discovery of ten "Troys", one built on top of another through the ages.

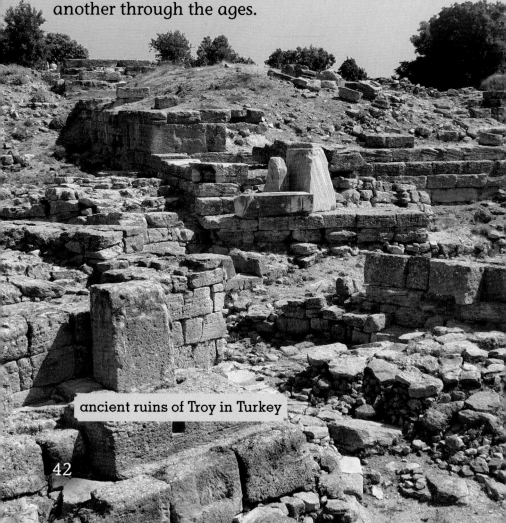

ancient ruins of Troy in Turkey

Remember – there's 80% of our oceans still to discover. So maybe there is still hope that, one day, someone will find the Lost City of Atlantis.

What do you think?

artist's impression of Atlantis

Glossary

archaeologists people who dig in the ground to find things from the past

BCE Before Common Era – before the year that Jesus was believed to have been born

crops fruit and vegetables grown to eat

earthquakes when the surface of the earth shakes

eroded when something is worn down over time

floods lots of water moving into an area that's usually dry

harbour a safe area of water where boats can be kept

invaders people who attack a place

malaria disease spread by mosquitoes

mosaics pictures made from small, colourful pieces of stone

prehistoric very old – before anything was written down

tidal wave massive wave in the sea

Index

Is Atlantis real?

Imagine that you have to convince someone that Atlantis is a real place. Which place would you choose to tell them about? What would be your argument for why this is the real Atlantis?

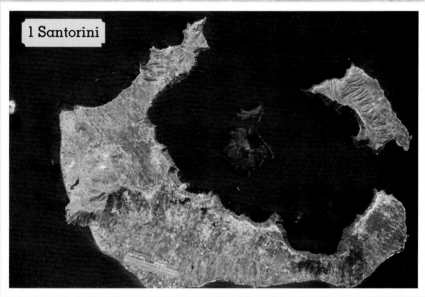

1 Santorini

2 Malta